NOVALIS

Yearning for Christmas

Christmas changes us –
and so it should.
More than that, we know
that it should.

Even today, when our lives have become frenzied dashes to complete a never-ending list of tasks — fuelled by the incessant demands to buy and consume, to achieve and compete — we yearn for a different kind of Christmas.

We want Christmas to be the antidote to our crazy lives; to be something more than all we can buy or accomplish. In fact, we want Christmas to fill that hole in our heart – a space that aches for God.

We know this, and at the same time we don't. Each year as Christmas approaches, the tension inside us begins to build. It is a tension that is fuzzy around the edges.

Our hearts call us to seek something that we vaguely perceive as the Christmas spirit. It smacks of good cheer, hospitality, compassion for the poor and the stranger, warmth towards our family and friends. But our minds don't listen all that well to our hearts.

Our minds listen to the world instead. And the world tells us we can only satisfy this yearning by buying things. If we buy the hottest new digital toy, the most expensive trinket or the grandest fashion statement for our nearest and dearest, we will feel loved.

If we frantically pull off the ultimate in chic holiday parties, complete with the trendiest cocktails and the most intricate gourmet delights, we will have "done Christmas" right. Or if we lavish our savings on an all-in-one exclusive Caribbean getaway, that ill-defined hunger will stop gnawing at our souls.

Can Christmas change us?

A las, the world's approach to Christmas leaves us hungry still for that elusive something. Too many of us finish the season exhausted, stressed out and irritated with everyone and everything. Our bank accounts are depleted, and for what?

The celebrations that we hoped would leave us warm inside, full of goodwill for all, have failed us. We feel emptier than ever.

Such Christmases do not change us – at least not for the better. This surprises us, but it shouldn't. Yet for those of us who do listen to our hearts, Christmas can indeed change our lives.

For centuries, the truth about Christmas has been right in front of us. We celebrate it still, in the religious festivities that are a legacy from our ancestors in faith.

In our worship lies the real food that can satisfy our hunger.

In those days, a decree went out from Emperor Augustus that all the world should be registered.
(Luke 2:1)

Some two thousand years ago, Christmas came upon a people in a tiny land in a faroff corner of the Roman Empire.

Even then, many people were busy and distracted; they yearned for something more. Christmas happened, and the world was changed.

Christmas came in the form
of a baby born to a teenage
girl named Mary, who was
betrothed but not yet married
to a carpenter named Joseph.
It was census time and they
had to travel to Joseph's
ancestral home of Bethlehem
to be counted.

But when they got to Bethlehem, there was no place to stay. Instead, the anxious couple took shelter in a stable. Jesus was born in that humble place.

No room in the inn

Who were these innkeepers who had no room for this young couple whose baby was about to be born? No doubt the innkeepers were busy people. Lots of people were coming to town, clamouring for lodging and food and having the money to pay for it.

Those innkeepers were desperately trying to meet all these demands and keep all their customers happy. They played an important role in their communities and had reputations to uphold. They only had room for so many.

In the end, they had jobs to do and mouths to feed.

Just like many of us.

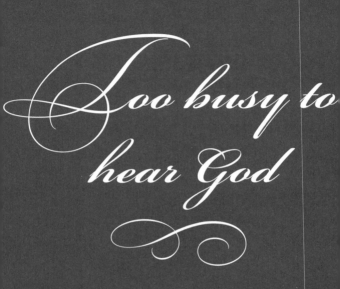

Too busy to
hear God

No doubt they were so busy, they couldn't hear God's messengers who were bringing "good news of great joy for all the people." And all – from the lowliest shepherds in the land to the wisest men of the age – heard this joyful message. Even King Herod himself heard the rumours that a king had been born. And didn't like what he heard.

It is interesting to note who listened to the messengers.

The shepherds in the hills of Judea tending their flocks paid attention.

They were among the poorest and least powerful in their land. They worried constantly about keeping wild animals from ravaging their sheep. They struggled to stay awake through the night, fighting the cold and boredom in equal measure.

But they heard the news.
An angel told them, "To you
is born this day in the city
of David a Saviour, who is
the Messiah, the Lord."
(Luke 2:11)

And right away the shepherds went to find this "child wrapped in bands of cloth and lying in a manger." Then they fell to praising God for what they had seen and heard. Their lives were never the same again.

Who are today's shepherds?
They are the ones who feel
the yearning in their hearts
and know that it is God
speaking to them. The ones
who know the answer to this
hunger isn't found in passing
pleasures, in consumer goods
or on the Internet.

How do we become more
like them?

The magi, too, got the message and listened. They followed a star in the east till they came upon that same infant, lying in humble surroundings. These wise men were rich, by the standards of their day, and offered gifts to this baby – gold, frankincense and myrrh. Gifts fit for a king!

What they didn't do was even more important. On their way to visit Jesus, they had enjoyed the hospitality of King Herod. The jealous king, thinking this new "king" was born to overthrow him, slyly encouraged the wise men to fulfill their quest and then let him know where to find the baby Jesus, so Herod could pay him homage, too.

But Herod had no intention of paying him homage. Instead, he wanted to kill this child and destroy the threat to his own power. But the wise men would not play his game; after being warned in a dream not to reveal anything to Herod, they went home by another route, thwarting Herod's plan.

The Evangelist Matthew tells us that when the wise men saw Jesus, they "knelt down and paid him homage." (Matthew 2:11) The great ones of the world bowed down before an infant.

Who are our wise men and women today? Who are our farsighted leaders, those people who are not distracted by earthly luxuries – riches, pleasure, power? Who are the people who have achieved much by the world's standards, yet whose hearts remain open to the least among us? Who learn from these little ones and are changed forever?

Joseph
listens

Joseph is a most intriguing
man, a humble carpenter.
Throughout the gospels,
Joseph never says a word.
But he does something that
is all too rare – he listens to
his heart.

When the world tells Joseph that it is scandalous for him to take a pregnant Mary as his wife, Joseph listens instead to an angel in a dream, who tells him the child she bears is the Son of God. Joseph obeys God and provides a home for his family, a husband for Mary, and a father for Jesus.

When an angel warns Joseph in another dream that Herod wants to kill this child, Joseph obeys again, taking the family to Egypt and safety. And when Joseph is told, once more, by an angel in a dream that it is safe to return home with his family, he does just that.

Changed by
Christmas

It must have been terribly confusing and difficult for such a practical man – a man of the world – to listen to dreams and voices in his head. Far easier to quietly break his engagement to this questionable young woman and carry on with his simple life. Yet he knew when his heart was telling him the truth. Joseph was changed by Christmas.

Why we need people like Joseph

Who would want to be Joseph in our times? Today, we are urged to push ourselves to the front of the crowd, to beat the competition, be the best singer, dancer, comedian, banker, lawyer or accountant. Quiet people, who know the truth can't be bought, don't win grand prizes. But the Lord knows (and this is not just a figure of speech) that we need them.

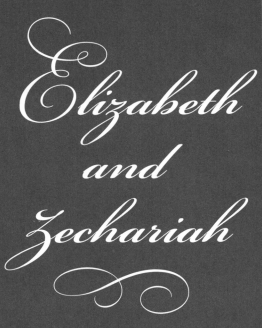

Elizabeth
and
Zechariah

Other characters in the gospels were changed by Christmas, even if they were not at the manger's side. Zechariah and Elizabeth, the elderly couple who became parents to John the Baptist, were privileged to be part of God's plan. They listened to God's messenger and joyfully obeyed. Their lives were never the same afterwards.

Simeon and Anna

Nor can we forget Simeon and Anna. They played bit parts in the lives of the Holy Family. When Jesus was brought to the temple in Jerusalem for the ritual offering of a sacrifice, Simeon was there.

This old man, righteous and devout, recognized in Jesus the Lord's anointed. Luke tells us how Simeon took the child in his arms and blessed God for allowing him to see the salvation of the world before Simeon died.

Anna, a widow who prayed daily in the temple, also saw Jesus for what he was. "At that moment she came, and began to praise God and to speak about the child to all who were looking for the redemption of Jerusalem." (Luke 2:38)

Listening to our elders today

Today's elderly are rarely the ones we look to for wisdom. We prefer to warehouse them out of sight, to keep them calm and quiet. We don't think they have much to contribute. A lot of them aren't even online!

Yet they are the keepers of our cultural memory; storehouses of a kind of knowledge that marks us out as human. Not even Google can replace this kind of memory.

Where in today's world do we find Zechariah and Elizabeth, Simeon and Anna? And will we let them teach us what they know?

Mary,
mother of God

No one was changed more by Christmas than Mary, the mother of Jesus.

What young teenager today could handle this otherworldly challenge? Yet Mary had a heart big enough to help her through all that lay ahead.

Not only that, she was filled with joy at the prospect! "My soul magnifies the Lord, and my spirit rejoices in God my Saviour," she proclaimed to her cousin Elizabeth (Luke 1:47).

Yet what a fearful burden it must have been at times: Who was this child she was carrying? How would Joseph react? Where would they live?

What would the future hold
for this son of hers, whom
everyone said was so special:
shepherds, wise men, elders
in the temple? How could
she bear this responsibility
and joy?

So many questions; so few answers. Scripture says Mary "pondered" in her heart these things that would befall her and her son. Throughout her life – when Jesus revealed his divine origins in his miracles, when he was condemned, tortured and crucified by those who feared and hated him – she continued to trust the words of the Angel Gabriel, who announced the looming birth of her son.

She turned all these things over in prayer, leaving it all to God, trusting in God's plan for the world.

In her faith and obedience,
Mary became much more than
just a model of behaviour for the
rest of us. Her complete and
total gift of herself to God
became a gift for the rest of us.
A gift that reminds us, again
and again, that Christmas can
transform our lives.

But how? Surely the Christmas story can no longer work its transformational magic. Our world is too cynical, too materialistic, too secular to let into our hearts this story about a baby born in a stable two thousand years ago.

Can we hear the story?

C an we even begin to really hear the story today? Hasn't Christmas itself been changed beyond all recognition? Is it truly possible to hear the angels sing?

Making
room for God

Yes, it is possible. We really can let Christmas into our hearts. Before we can do this, however, we must learn the lesson of Elijah.

Elijah the prophet, seeking to hear the voice of God, stood on a mountain and listened.

A great wind passed, then an
earthquake and fire, but God
wasn't in any of these.
Instead, God came in
"a sound of sheer silence."
(1 Kings 19:12)

It is not in the loudest noise of our Christmas celebrations that we will find a truth to change our hearts. It is in the silence.

Seeking silence in a noisy world

Winter, especially our northern winter, lends itself well to fostering silence. The deep, long, dark nights of December speak to our internal longing. Advent itself, those four weeks of preparation for the coming of Emmanuel, provide the opportunity. If we allow ourselves the chance, we can find the silence we need to hear that still, small voice of God.

In Advent, our liturgies point to "preparing the way" for our hearts, urging us to find time for prayer and the internal exercise our souls need to truly be changed by Christmas. There is genius in the tradition of midnight Mass – set in the stillness of that special night, it forces us to clear our minds of the commercial clutter of our too-hectic lives and give ourselves over to the ultimate Gift.

If we let it, this special Eucharist will provide a clear path into the Christmas story for both our hearts and our minds.

Let us allow our hearts to walk the path the Holy Family trod, from inn to inn, finally settling for the night in a lowly stable. Let us remember how the innkeepers, in their busyness, reflect our own lives today. Let us be overwhelmed, as the shepherds were, at the angelic messengers. And, like the wise men, let us kneel in awe before the divine majesty of a tiny babe.

Then let us put ourselves in Joseph's sandals and live with him the wrenching decisions he faced. Let us recall the joy and gratitude of Simeon and Anna. Most of all, let us ponder with Mary this miraculous thing that happened long ago in the still, silent darkness of Bethlehem.

Yes, Christmas can change us. It can open our hearts to the entire world, which is filled with the glory of God.

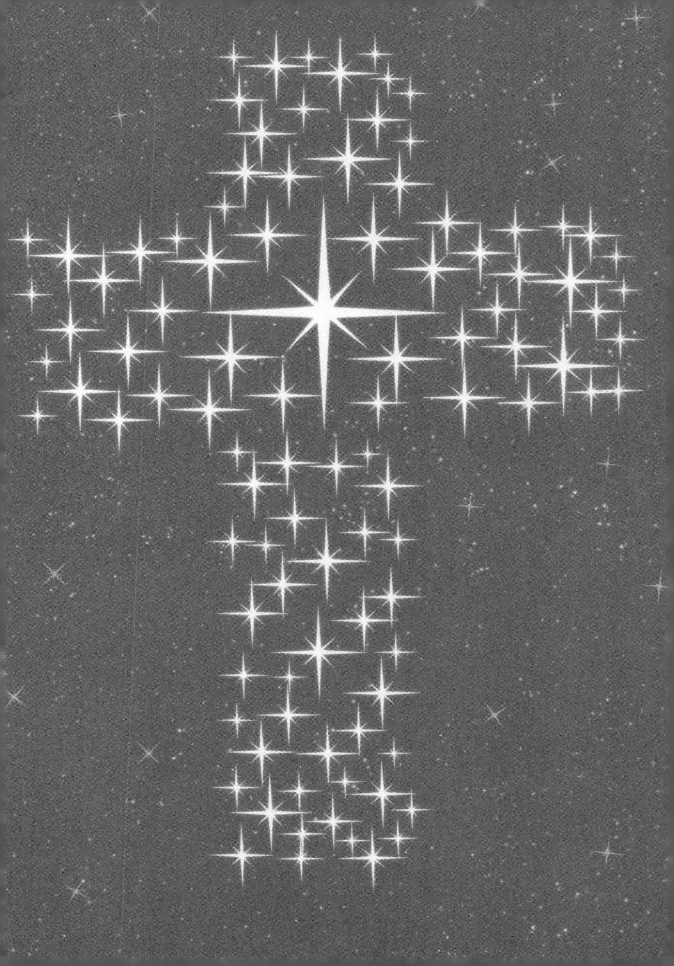

© 2012 Novalis Publishing Inc.

Cover: Quatre-Quarts
Cover photo: Crestock.com
Layout: Danielle Dugal and Amy Eaton
Interior photos: Crestock.com, except the
following: 15: Jupiter images; 24–25, 36–37: Novalis;
56–57, 102–103: Plaisted; 74–75: Jocelyn Boutin

Published by Novalis

Publishing Office
10 Lower Spadina Avenue, Suite 400
Toronto, Ontario, Canada
M5V 2Z2

Head Office
4475 Frontenac Street
Montréal, Québec, Canada
H2H 2S2

www.novalis.ca

Library and Archives Canada Cataloguing in Publication

Sinasac, Joseph P. (Joseph Patrick), 1957-
Christmas / Joseph Patrick Sinasac.

(Faith moments)
ISBN 978-2-89646-468-5

1. Christmas. I. Title. II. Series: Faith moments

BV45.S54 2012   242'.335   C2012-901603-9

Printed in Canada.

We acknowledge the financial support of the Government
of Canada through the Canada Book Fund for business
development activities.

5   4   3   2   1   16   15   14   13   12